How to Talk to Santa

BY ALEC GREVEN

ILLUSTRATIONS BY KEI ACEDERA

Collins
An Imprint of HarperCollinsPublishers

For my grandparents: Ree Ree and Papa, Opa and Nana.
Also for Oma and Papa Tim, who are with me in my heart.

Collins is an imprint of HarperCollins Publishers.

How to Talk to Santa
Text copyright © 2009 by Alec Greven
Illustrations copyright © 2009 by Kei Acedera

Printed in the United States of America.

Library of Congress Cataloging-in-Publication Data
Greven, Alec.
    How to talk to Santa / by Alec Greven ; Illustrations by Kei Acedera.
      p.   cm.
    ISBN 978-0-06-180207-2 (trade bdg.)
    1. Santa Claus. 2. Christmas. I. Acedera, Kei, ill. II. Title.
GT4985.G74 2009   2009020548
394.2663—dc22   CIP
                                      AC

Typography by Ray Shappell
09 10 11 12 13 LP/WOR 10 9 8 7 6 5 4 3 2
❖ First Edition

CONTENTS

INTRODUCTION

Ever wonder about the big guy in the red suit?
You know . . . Santa!

There are many signs that Christmas is almost here and Santa is
on his way—lights everywhere, Christmas trees in all the windows,
and toys, toys, toys! It's easy for kids to go wild at Christmas.

But Christmas is not just about toys and wanting everything you
see. It's about having fun and believing in magic, getting together
and giving to others.

So, how do you control your greed, still get what you want, and
spread the cheer? Read this book and find out, because Santa is
almost here!

CHAPTER ONE

The Countdown

{ *Operation Christmas begins right after Thanksgiving.* }

Operation Christmas (OC) begins right after Thanksgiving. One day everything is normal, and then all of a sudden people get zapped with OC and go crazy. Everyone starts shopping, decorating, and having parties. Some people go a little overboard, if you know what I mean.

You know Christmas is coming when . . .
- ✔ "Jingle Bells" is stuck in your head.
- ✔ Giant snow globes and dancing Santas take over your yard.
- ✔ Every commercial on TV makes you want new toys.

Kids get into the spirit by starting the Christmas countdown, making decorations, breaking out the Christmas stories and movies, and writing THE LIST for Santa.

That's when you know OC has hit you bad.

TIP: *98% of people do not do OC calmly.*

But one thing that doesn't get kids in the spirit is taking Christmas pictures. This turns your parents into aliens. First, they make you wear clothes that match your brother's and sister's, and usually it is something fancy and uncomfortable. And who wants to match your four-year-old sister anyway?

Then you have to pose until your legs go to sleep or you get an itch, and your sister keeps poking you.

Many kids will put on a goofy face or not look at the camera. But Mom and Dad will be mad if you do this. They expect you to smile while your brother is stepping on your foot. 94% of the time someone messes up the picture and you have to do it over and over again.

This is too much for some kids. I have never taken Christmas pictures without a kid breaking down into tears.
Happy Christmas Pictures!

TIP: *Keep in mind it is drama time. Just fake it and get through it.*

CHAPTER TWO

Being Naughty

{ *We don't know how he knows. . . . So watch out.* }

Santa watches your behavior the whole year. But December is the most important time not to be naughty. This is when Santa pays *extra* attention to everything you do.

Now, everybody makes mistakes, and Santa isn't going to cross you off his list for one problem. You are probably okay if you are good 75% of the time.

But Santa sees everything, all the time! Even if you don't get caught, Santa knows.

TIP: *There's no safe time for pranks around Christmas.*

We don't know how he knows. He might have spies, or your parents might tell, or it might just be his magic. So watch out.

Naughty things that could get you into Santa-trouble:

✔ Putting soap in your brother's juice
✔ Hiding your sister's dolls
✔ "Accidentally" knocking your brother into a puddle
✔ Whining

TIP: *Don't whine now; whine later. The day after Christmas is National Whiners' Day.*

Some kids think it's okay to be naughty right after Christmas because you already got your presents and probably Santa is too tired to pay attention for next year.

Caution! You are not in the safe zone. This is actually a risky time.

After Christmas you have brand-new toys that your parents can take away if you are not having good behavior!

CHAPTER THREE

Being Nice

{ *You can't fool Santa.* }

On January 1, you have a mission: Try to be good all year. It's really hard, but you have to keep your eye on the prize at the end.

You might want to come up with a strategy to avoid temptation, so you don't fall into trouble and make Santa skip your house. You have to give it some real thought first and then put your niceness plan into action.

Here are some things you can do:

- ✓ Eliminate backtalk.
- ✓ Impress your parents by doing what they ask plus more.
- ✓ Help a lot more around the house, but don't make it obvious that you are working for presents.

Keep it casual for best results.

Don't be a double agent and just pretend to be nice. It's not going to work if you're only on good behavior in front of people but then do what you want behind their backs.

Sneaky stuff to avoid:

✓ Saying you cleaned your room when you didn't. That will never fool your parents.
✓ Bribing your sister to do your chores. That will make your mom mad.
✓ Playing a computer game when you say you're doing your homework. That will make your parents report you to Santa.

TIP: *You can't fake being nice. Santa knows if you are faking.*

CHAPTER FOUR

Making a List and Checking It Twice

{ *You want to make a good impression on Santa.* }

Project Wish List is very important and takes some planning because you want to make a good impression on Santa. The Christmas list is tricky because kids want everything, but you don't want Santa to think you are greedy and selfish.

95% of kids go overboard with their Christmas lists.

Making a list is like what you do in school. You have to draft, revise, and edit before it is ready.

Start out by listing every single thing you want. This is your draft.

Then cut back so your chances of getting what you want will be better. This is how you revise.

See if your brother will put some of your toys on his wish list. You have to convince him that he would like them. This is how you edit.

TIP: *Try this maneuver at your own risk! If your brother gets the toys you want for Christmas, he might claim them as his and not share. Backfire!*

When you are ready for your final list, make sure you start it politely. "May I please have" or "I am wishing for" is much better than "I want" or "I need."

Then it is persuasion time. Tell Santa why you want the toys and what is special about them. Emphasize things like it is good for family time or exercise. That seems to help.

Then send your letter to Santa and hope for the best!

Your wish list is like a ship. If you are greedy and overload it with toys, it will sink.

TIP: *To avoid greed, you should not watch too many toy commercials. They suck you in. The more you watch, the more you want.*

CHAPTER FIVE

Cookies, Carrots, and Christmas Eve

{ *The wait is almost over!* }

Christmas Eve means the wait is almost over! You are super excited and can't wait another minute. But hold your horses—you have to get ready for Santa.

On the big night, make sure your stocking is hung. Set out a thank-you letter and a treat for Santa. Also, don't forget the reindeer! Leave something special for them too, like carrots.

Don't freak out if you don't have a chimney. Santa will just come through the door.

Now it's time to get serious. When it's bedtime, don't argue.
You might get to stay up later than normal, but you have to go to
bed or Santa won't come. That's a fact.

And don't stall or whine—it makes your parents mad. Plus it makes
Santa's job harder. He has to deliver presents to every kid in the
world and can't do it if they're not asleep.

Some kids come up with a battle plan to try to catch Santa on Christmas Eve. You might think you can stay awake and sneak downstairs or hide behind the couch until he comes. But Santa won't come if you are awake or hiding. This is something else he knows. It is part of his magic. So don't bother.

TIP: *There is a 99.999999999% chance that you will never ever catch Santa. My advice is: Don't risk it!*

CHAPTER SIX

Santa Is Here!

{ *Try to contain your excitement.* }

Most kids wake up at 4 a.m. to open their presents, but then all they get are cranky parents. Try to contain your excitement until maybe 6 a.m. But a better time is 7 a.m. if you want totally cranky-free parents.

If you decide to go wake up your parents really early, send the youngest kid in first to test the waters.

When your parents get up, it doesn't mean presents right away.
You have to control yourself.

First parents have to get coffee. Then they have to get out the
video camera and then they want to take pictures *before* you
open the presents.

Finally you get to run downstairs and see if Santa came!

Then you open presents and eat cinnamon rolls and play with your family and your new things all day.

FACT: *There is nothing like Christmas morning!*

Even if you are extra excited, don't forget to be nice when opening your presents.

If you get a fuzzy purple sweater or a pair of ugly socks, don't say, "I'm not wearing these to school!" Say something like "Thank you!" or "I've always wanted these," even if it is not really true.

Then just move on and don't let it ruin your day.

TIP: *If you don't get what you want, don't pout. Put it on your list for next year.*

CHAPTER SEVEN

The Truth About Santa

{ *You can be 100 and still believe.* }

Toys and presents aren't the only good things about Christmas. Santa is more than just a mailman. He's all about giving and helping others, too.

You probably have heard that giving is better than receiving. Most kids don't agree.

But, once you start doing it, helping someone else makes you feel good.

Kids can help in a lot of ways:

✓ Collect cans of food to give away.
✓ Give a toy to a kid who really needs it.
✓ Donate a dollar to charity.

It doesn't seem like much, but if tons of people help in little ways, it will make a big difference! We can all be Santa at Christmas.

TIP: *If you have extra, share it with someone else. If you don't, hopefully someone will share with you.*

The real magic of Santa is not the presents. It is believing in the good everyone can do.

Santa is for every kid and every age.

You can be 100 and still believe.

ACKNOWLEDGMENTS

Thank you to the awesome people at
HarperCollins who believed in a kid and
helped me become a real author.
—Alec

*A generous donation has been made by Alec Greven and HarperCollins to support
Stand Up To Cancer, a program of the Entertainment Industry Foundation
to raise awareness and funds to accelerate groundbreaking cancer research.*